W.G. Hill
The Millionaire's Favourite Read

HOW TO BE A CONSULTANT

1st Edition – CONFIDENTIAL REGISTERED COPY
No.____
FOR USE OF ORIGINAL BUYER ONLY

HOW TO BE A CONSULTANT

As a consultant, you can operate from anywhere
and advise by e-mail or telephone.

Facts and Figures are Constantly Changing.
By the time you read this book, things might have changed.

For questions and further information, contact the publisher:

W.G Hill's OFFICIAL website:
PTsecrets WEB
Join our discussion forums for PT readers
- the PT Club and the PT Refuge -
You will find more details on the six flags,
the PT philosophy, and the PT books,
and plenty of free reading material at the
W.G Hill's OFFICIAL Site: PTsecrets WEB
< www.FreedomPrivacyWealth.com >

Published by FreedomPrivacyWealth.com
Edited by Dennis DeWitt
Cover Art by Dennis DeWitt
Co-author and updateds by "Grandpa"

HOW TO BE A CONSULTANT
Copyright ©
2020 FreedomPrivacyWealth.com

All rights reserved. No part of this book may be reproduced or transmitted in any form or by any means, electronic or mechanical, including photocopying and recording, or by any information storage or retrieval system without the publisher's written permission, except in the case of a reviewer, who may quote brief passages embodied in critical articles or in a review so long as credit is given to HOW TO BE A CONSULTANT by W.G. Hill and www.FreedomPrivacyWealth.com

While reliable sources have been sought out in compiling this book, neither the author, publisher, nor distributor can accept any liability for the accuracy of its contents nor for the consequences of any reliance placed upon it. Always consult a local professional before taking any risks.

ISBN: 9798558690712

About the Author

To Predict the Future – You Have to Know the Past!

YOU WON'T FIND W.G. Hill ON ANY BESTSELLER LISTS, BUT IT'S HARD TO FIND A MILLIONAIRE WHO HASN'T READ MOST OF HIS $100 "SPECIAL REPORTS."

Dr. W.G. Hill is the father of the PT concept. Hill is a former American citizen, entrepreneur, self-made millionaire, author, and inveterate traveler, was influenced by the concepts of Harry Schultz. He had found a winning formula on which to base his future. In 1979, after years of living a PT lifestyle and fine-tuning many new ideas, In 1985, Hill wrote the first definitive book on the subject, entitled "PT." This valuable work discusses the essence of the philosophy and is definitely recommended reading for Anyone who aspires to a free and uncompromising way of life.

Hill's Low Profile -- The name W.G. Hill isn't bandied around much in the book-publishing World. No literary society has ever discussed any of the two dozen or so volumes this author has produced. But over the last forty years, in the World of bankers, accountants, high net worth investors, and financiers with offshore interests, Hill has been a seminal influence.

His most famous book is PT, or "Perpetual Traveller." Though this title might convey the idea that it's a book about traveling, it isn't. The subject is how wealthy people can - with proper paperwork - enjoy life more. Its "How to have a good time with your money, but at the same time avoid unwelcome attention that conspicuous consumption and high profile wealth always bring." These negatives include the unwelcome intrusions of tax collectors, insurance salesman, contingent fee plaintiff's lawyers, alimony seeking ex-wives, kidnappers, burglars. Not to mention every description of con-man.

Do these matters concern millionaires? Judging from Hill's book sales, they do, indeed. One of his early fans was the newsletter guru, Sir Harry Schultz, who must have made enough beforehand or sold enough books to live well. (In 1964, Harry D. Schultz - the World's highest-paid financial consultant, according to "Guinness Book of World Records.")

Sir Harry writes in PT, "I spent my first few years as a tax exile at the Monte Carlo Beach Hotel, interacting with hard-bodied, high maintenance cost divorced women who in their topless bikinis populated Riviera pool sides like motes in the sunshine."

Hill's books always offered his personal services to assist any reader in accomplishing the goals set out. For instance, his 1975 Lloyd's Report promised the reader would "make serious money without any investment, work or risk." This was two decades before many Lloyd's names did, in fact, suffer substantial losses. But Hill wrote later, "If people handled their Lloyd's relationships as I suggested (with stop-loss insurance), they came out way ahead." Hill charged a hefty fee to introduce new names and get them into Lloyd's as insurance underwriters.

Eventually, around 1985, Hill's maneuvers were picked up and, after that, published by Nicholas Pine. Pine was then operating as Milestone Press of Plymouth, England. He was a minor publisher of books for collectors of ceramics. Their typical press run in the pre-Hill days was a thousand copies. With Hill's books for millionaires soon selling like hotcakes, Milestone hit pay dirt. Pine changed his company's name to Scope International.

An ex-employee revealed that sales of well over 100,000 copies of each Hill book would have been "a low ballpark figure at the time he quit." With ten books being major sellers and a direct mail price of $100 per book, that means that gross sales of Hill's books passed the 100 million dollar mark many years ago. As marketers who sell direct via advertising and junk-mail, that means most revenues go directly to the bottom line. Although book sales figures are not available to the public (through bookstores), this could mean that little known Scope, by publishing the works of a mystery man who disappeared years ago, is far and away, the World's most profitable book publisher.

But The Profits Just Start With Book Sales -- Each Hill report describes a certain product or lifestyle. If the reader wants to make it a reality, he hires Hill to get him up and run. The Hill books suggest other ways that millionaires can enjoy their money more - by spending it on "lifestyle-enhancing" products and services. PT and all of Hill's books' basic premise is that any wealthy person will enjoy life more and protect his assets better by using what Hill calls "five flags."

HOW TO BE A CONSULTANT
Reviews & Ratings for W.G. Hills Previous Work

Rating details

☆☆☆☆☆ 34,157 ratings
4.52 out of 5 stars

5 ☆ ▇▇▇▇▇▇▇▇▇▇ 40% (16,752)
4 ☆ ▇▇▇▇▇▇▇▇ 33% (13,865)
3 ☆ ▇▇▇▇▇ 19% (7,931)
2 ☆ ▇ 5% (2,167)
1 ☆ | 3% (1,077)

Book ratings by booktopia.live

Banking in Silence:

Amazon Customer
☆☆☆☆☆ **Five Stars**
March 22, 2017

Format : Hardcover | Verified Purchase
Excellent!

Mirth Deshler
☆☆☆☆☆ **Very nice book**
April 14, 2019

Format : Hardcover | Verified Purchase

Coolbrieze
☆☆☆☆☆ **Must Have for the Private Individuals and Survivalists**
May 21, 2011

Format : Hardcover | Verified Purchase

Think Like a Tycoon

Amazon Customer
☆☆☆☆☆ **Five Stars**
November 16, 2015

Format : Paperback | Verified Purchase
Great book to read

Oceans Equity Group
☆☆☆☆☆ **How To Make Money 101 - Must Read**
July 2, 2018

Format : Paperback | Verified Purchase

Michael "MG" Gilson
☆☆☆☆☆ **Underground Classic on Real Estate Investing**
Reviewed in the United States on June 21, 2000

The Passport Report

A. Stephens

☆☆☆☆☆ **The Passport Report W. G. Hill**
June 28, 2017

Format : Hardcover | Verified Purchase

The Lloyds Report

Randall Layman

☆☆☆☆☆ **their is still great information**
September 15, 2015

Format : Hardcover | Verified Purchase

PT 2 The Practice

Amazon Customer

☆☆☆☆☆ **Five Stars**
March 22, 2017

Format : Hardcover | Verified Purchase
Excellent!

PT

 Michael T.

☆☆☆☆☆ **The Holy Bible of the Individualist**
October 25, 2011

Format : Hardcover | Verified Purchase

 Irish74

☆☆☆☆☆ **Five Stars**
October 23, 2014

Format : Hardcover
Good copy, well packaged. Thanks.

 ScottyMac

☆☆☆☆☆ **Dated, but good**
March 21, 2012

Format : Hardcover | Verified Purchase

 John Galt

☆☆☆☆☆ **One of the most impactful books on my entire life!**
June 28, 2015

Eric Sandoval rated it ★★★★★   May 26, 2014

This is without a doubt one of THE greatest books I have ever read. It is a philosophy that I seek to attain as a personal lifestyle.

2 likes · Like · see review

Randall Layman rated it ★★★★★   Dec 11, 2016

The moment I received this book, I could not put it down. It changed my whole philosophy of life and world view. While some aspects of the book may be outdated, the underlying philosophy of self-responsibility and individualism regardless of your place on the planet is unchanged.

Dedication

To those who inspired me to write this book

Acknowledgments

My editor Dennis DeWitt
My cover artist and designer Dennis DeWitt
"Grandpa" co-author for providing updates.
The Readers who said my work was better.

PT books by DR. W.G. Hill J.D.
(Author, Investigator, and Consultant)

The following W. G. Hill PT Collection – Timeless PT Classics has been updated or is available again in its original version.

THE MONACO REPORT
THE CAMPIONE REPORT
PT "Perpetual Traveller"
THINK LIKE A TYCOON
INSIDER SECRETS
LE LIVRE DU CORPS DIPLOMATIQUE
"How You Can Become An Honorary Consul General"
THE PASSPORT REPORT

[originals out of print]
PT 1
A Coherent Plan for a Stress-Free, Healthy and Prosperous Life Without Government Interference, Taxes or Coercion J
PT 2
The Practice – Freedom and Privacy Tactics
Channel Island Report
How to Acquire a Tax Haven Domicile in the Channel Islands for Fifty Pounds Per Month
Computer Privacy Report
How PTs in Cyberspace Make Money in Secret
The Andorra and Gibraltar Report
Undiscovered Fiscal Paradises of the Iberian Peninsula
The Lloyds Report
How to earn substantial offshore income without the investment of time or money.
The Albania Report
Banking in Silence
The Complete Manual on How to Protect Your Money
The Tax-Free Car Report
How To Own A New Luxury Car Every Year Free, For Life

HOW TO BE A CONSULTANT

For many years the author was a successful consultant. Consulting is an excellent "Portable Trade." You can do from anywhere on Earth, online, and without any permits or government licenses.

If you want to be a highly paid, sought after consultant with more business than you can handle, there are several things to keep in mind:

Your Product?
You must have (or you will need to gain) some special knowledge [expertise]. People must want what you know enough to be willing to pay you for imparting information and guidance.

Marketing

You have to spread the word that what you have to sell is worthwhile and good value for money. This step, otherwise known as "marketing to your target market," is something you must get right. Without good marketing, you will have no clients and no income. For some free marketing tips (and a pitch to take his advanced seminars,) google "Jay Abrahams." He is a marketing consultant who gives advice to many businesses and also gives $20,000@ seminars. He reportedly makes well over $4 million per year. I met him when he started his career as a consultant with local classified advertisements offering his services to sell any product or service. He asked for a 50% contingent fee of new profits he brought in. Later in this article, I will mention other sources of marketing ideas.

Client Service

You must be both discrete and highly dependable. You must deliver the information and benefits as promised, on time. When your customers need you urgently, you must be there for them. No excuses. You must respect confidentiality. Your clients won't want their private affairs broadcast to the World, nor to ANYONE!

ATTRACTING CUSTOMERS

One of the best ways to attract customers is to write an attention-grabbing article or better, a book about your subject. After all, "The Man Who Wrote the Book" is always thought to be the expert. You can promote your book on radio and TV talk shows, via news articles in Magazines and newspapers, Internet Blogs, advertising, and on Internet websites like Google or YouTube. Simply listing your book on a site like Amazon.com won't, in and of itself, sell any books or get you any clients.

Of all the marketing methods, I've found that TV interview shows are, by far, the most effective. Radio talk shows are second, and a favorable buzz from reviews and word of mouth on the Internet are third. I'd put classified ads as 4th. A favorable recommendation is more important than advertising because with the endorsement of a trusted source, strangers will have more confidence in you. Anyone can advertise and say most anything. But if Oprah Winfrey says (on her popular TV show) that she believes in you, your place on the bestseller list is almost assured. It is easier than you think to get on local radio talk shows-for instance. You just call the station, tell them what you want to talk about, and usually, you get booked on a late night or early morning show. Be articulate and show enthusiasm. If the show producers like you, you will get referrals to many other shows with better time slots.

There are many good books on how to promote yourself. Read a few ideas. Try different techniques—experiment and use what works. If you have more money than time, you can hire an effective "public relations consultant" to get your name and info about your services out to the public. Maybe they will work for you on a contingent fee. No results, no pay. Once you have some clients, your customers (if you are any good) will also recommend you. Ultimately, customer satisfaction and word of mouth referrals are your best sales tool.

Whether (as a Consultant) you just advise or also "implement" is up to you. Implementation would involve interacting with others on behalf of your client. This can be immensely time-consuming. Lawyers and accountants are consultants. I don't like either of them much because their main objective is usually to keep you on the hook, paying regular retainer fees. To defend yourself in a lawsuit, keep your account books, or run an active business, you may need lawyers and accountants. PTs, of course, don't generally need either lawyers or accountants.

For some people, especially those who are highly visible, make many deals, and/or operate on the edge of the law, lawyers are probably needed to keep you out of trouble. Unfortunately, most of these "Licensed Professionals" want to keep you dependent- a "cash cow" paying them as long as you live. Further, they put their interests first. You are in second place. In my experience, most medical doctors, CPAs, and lawyers try to make you believe that you can't live without them. But you can. Too often, they make you think you must pay them regularly to keep yourself physically and financially healthy. They turn you into a supplicant/dependant. It is best if you can handle your own affairs without depending on them blindly.

Sometimes medical doctors or lawyers are necessary [to set a broken leg or settle a claim, for instance]. But too often, they just make healthy people believe they need them for every minor complaint. They can [like lawyers and accountants] get in the way of a permanent solution because they want to be paid regularly. As a PT., you don't need them anymore. You can solve your problems once and for all and move on to a more productive, happier life.

My personal view is that the sooner you can extricate yourself from the clutches of lawyers, accountants, bureaucrats, and most medical doctors, the better off you will be.

With my consulting clients, I intend, after a couple of PT learning years with me, that they will end up confident, financially independent, and able to take complete control of their lives. I teach them to be self-confident in their own abilities and how to become as competent as I am. (Hopefully MORE competent than I am!)

One PT goal should have a Portable Trade or Profession that can be used to earn money anywhere-without any bureaucratic licensing worries. Becoming a consultant is ideal for this.

Most of the process of being a top-notch consultant involves giving the client confidence, passing on your experience and expertise, then, before you part company, explaining and teaching where to find further specialized information and advice.

Unlike many professionals, I don't try to make anyone dependent on me. I want anyone who comes within my orbit to be able to handle their own problems quickly. Life, I feel, should be a do-it-yourself project. If my ex-clients choose to become a competitor-consultant on PT matters or otherwise, I am not jealous. I only hope that they will pass on the best of what they've learned from me to their clients. There is enough business out there to satisfy everyone.

For me, social friendships with ex-clients and later, information sharing based on equality and "no pay" are the best consultants, and I should aim for and achieve.

DON'T GIVE THEM A FISH; TEACH THEM HOW TO FISH!

My approach (and what I recommend for you) reveals your clients their hidden options-moves they probably never considered.

The most basic PT example is that by merely leaving any given jurisdiction and internationalizing, one gets rid of lawsuits, government problems, and a restricted outlook. Like a good music teacher, I never resent it when my clients achieve competence and can be left to navigate independently. If they become PT Consultants and compete with me—I like it because it means I have done my job well. There is, in fact, a shortage of good advice and guidance.

In short order, my clients become their own Doctors, Lawyers, and Accountants- plus just about everything else. Most clients' first step is overcoming their irrational fears, scraping all past burdens, legal problems, debts, social obligations, and any unwarranted dread of the unknown.

A PORTABLE PROFESSION?

As a consultant, you can operate from anywhere and advise by e-mail or telephone. One of my best friends charges $3000 for a quarter-hour telephone call or e-mail. Due to time restraints, he turns away more client inquiries than he accepts. Personal contact can be reserved for your high net worth, most exciting clients. Usually, clients will either come to you or pay for your first class travel to see them. Client contacts are generally very stimulating and can be great fun. Sometimes they result in very profitable business opportunities. Having a few consulting clients (plus another business) keeps you focused and on your toes. You never stop learning.

HOW TO BEGIN

Where do you start? Common sense! If you are not already an expert with a Ph. D. in your topic, become a self-made master. How? Read books on the subject you wish to be an expert on. Then, get practical experience. You must first do whatever it is you aim to be an expert on. Learn from your mistakes and later, from the mistakes of your clients. Ensure that your next client won't make the same wrong turns that you [or they] did.

As time goes by, you will inevitably become better and better, just like the surgeon who does the same operation many times over.

CONSIDER WRITING A BOOK TO PROMOTE YOUR BUSINESS

Even if a book or newsletter is done only for the back end business it produces, it may be worthwhile to do it. A loss leader, as it is called in the trade, is something that brings in customers. It can be something given away as a gift or sold at a loss. A book that establishes you as an expert on any subject is a major asset for anyone to have.

If writing a book is too formidable a task, consider this: When you write regular articles for a newsletter, at the end of a year, you will have enough interesting material to fill up a book. Many of your own newsletter subscribers will buy this book if only to have your pearls of wisdom in a permanent form. A book is an inevitable result when you, as a journalist (and that's what you are as a newsletter writer), do a series of articles on similar theses or related topics.

The newsletter usually comes before the book but not necessarily...

YOUR FIRST PUBLICATION NEED NOT BE A BOOK

But get something in print that will serve as your calling card. Write a Book-or at least a Pamphlet. Call it "A Special Report on XYZ." You might be able to convince an editor to write a regular column in a newspaper or magazine. One of my favorite columnists is Walt Mossberg. He writes about the Internet, software, and communication gadgets for the Wall Street Journal. He also has an online blog. If he were a consultant for hire, I'd undoubtedly use him for any assistance needed in that area of expertise.

Advice columns or daily spots on radio programs are very successfully used as business builders. Another lady I knew, Ann Landers, along with her daughter Margo (see Slate.com), and her twin sister "Dear Abbey" all had "lovelorn" columns that started small and locally. They became very popular and widely syndicated. Their weekly columns made money. Public speaking engagements (speaking to groups) paid even better.

Result? Some consultants never give 'one to one' advice. It is because they enjoy personal contact, like me, that they do personal consulting on a limited basis.

Later, by summarizing the client's problems and the resolutions that worked, you can revise and expand your special reports. One or more special reports can become a book or even a multi-volume set. Do as I did with Bye Bye Big Brother, a $500 three-volume set [now sold out except for a few copies in my personal library] that one reviewer described as "the millionaire's favorite read."

Virtually all of my new clients were/are BBBB readers. In fact, I insist they become familiar with BBBB so that we don't waste any time re-iterating the PT basics.

Once you write about any endeavor field, you will end up with more useful information than you can ever get into print. High net worth clients who read your books or reports will want your general information personally tailored to fit them. The same people who buy one-of-a-kind apparel and original artworks expect to pay more for personal consulting. And of course, you/we can't put some of our best tips into print for legal or other reasons. Another reason is that if any technique is too widely known and practiced, it is no longer as effective.

HOW DID IT ALL START FOR ME?

At the risk of breaking your heart, here's my story: I was heartbroken, lonely, and almost broke- having been dumped and divorced by my movie starlet "trophy" wife. She had me evicted from our own home, then got a court order to keep all my bank accounts, houses, cars, the horses, and the kids. I couldn't even see the kids without a man-hating lesbian social worker in attendance. My babies were brainwashed to cry and carry on every time I came into their lives- making any 'joint custody' visits intolerable. The divorce proceedings were degrading- surely the lowest point in my life.

At the same time that my ex was grabbing all my assets, two other previous wives were also suing for more support. As I wouldn't (or couldn't) pay them all, I was tossed into the hoosegow for "contempt." There, confined to the "tank," with a bunch of drunks and slobs, I thought long and hard: I knew I had to make a change. That is when I planned an Escape from America.

I thought up a primitive version of the PT life for myself. It was simple:

I simply got on a bus (untraceable) and exited. I was inspired by cowboy movies where the outlaws went "South of the Border, Down Mexico Way." In other words, I hit the road and got myself out of a jurisdiction where I had problems. It was not easy to face the unknown because I didn't have any guru [like I am now] to hold my hand. Yet this move to a new life was probably the best decision I ever made.

Without me as a defendant, the pending divorce and alimony cases evaporated insofar as I was concerned. I got myself a new (foreign) identity and passport. It was easier then, pre 9-11, but a new identity is still legally do-able. The "old me" didn't exist anymore. For the first time in my life, I was debt-free, single again- and free of all social and moral obligations to anyone.

I soon found ways of legally making more money; tax-free than I had ever done before.

It seemed to me that similar and easy solutions to my problems could be sold to others in the same position. There had to be many individuals who were sick and tired of being harassed by the Government or being defendants in never-ending the litigation. For many reasons, I figured that people wanted to break out of their rut and start a new life – maybe with a new identity.

The late Harry Brown's book, How I Found Freedom In An Unfree World, was good inspiration. But ultimately, my main inspiration came from Harry Schultz. His books, writings, and personal advice (that I paid for) gave me a path to follow and helped me become the PT [Perpetual Traveler] I am today.

I quickly realized that the 6 PT Flags could be used by anyone who had similar problems to mine. Those who would break out of their rut and use the six PT flags (see FreedomPrivacyWealth.com) were almost always going to be people who had to escape from looming problems. Of course, to enjoy the PT way of life, you don't need to wait for a crisis. At a stroke, anyone can escape, make more money, enjoy great unlimited sex, pay no taxes, travel, be debt-free, and even become incredibly healthy.

To make a fresh start, you just have to leave where you are.

Strange- how most people are afraid to make the first move! Many individuals are so desperate that they contemplate or commit suicide. They never realize that by hoisting even one of the 6 PT Flags, they'll instantly enjoy a far more pleasant, life-affirming way forward.

THE FIRST STOP

Early on, in Tijuana (Mexico) bars and later, Pattaya (Thailand), I met many happy PTs. A few were financial fugitives escaping, often from a criminal frame-up or sting. Many were alimony evaders. They had no "PT" label for the life they were leading.

Theirs was a kind of happy escape from their first world home country to the 2nd or 3rd World. This was a path many had discovered, yet before 1985, no one had ever written about it.

Soon, from Belize, an English speaking country below Mexico, I was busy helping other men in a similar position (and a few women too) leave their home countries to start new lives abroad. As PTs, they could avoid all contacts with courts, cops, bureaucrats, plaintiffs, stalkers, ex-spouses, and other troublemakers.

Belize (at the time) offered an easy-to-get 2nd passport that was good for travel all over the World and for getting residence almost anywhere. These Belize "investor passports," priced retail at $50,000, were particularly saleable in Hong Kong and Taiwan. For those in the know, you didn't have to spend serious money to get one. The same Belize passport was available for a few hundred dollars by establishing a legitimate residence there [then, traveling anywhere], and waiting for the clock to run on the required couple of years.

MY FIRST LITERARY EFFORTS

I became a serious PT consultant by writing a few predecessors to the BBBB book. They were not books really, just short "Special Reports." The first was about escaping from problems like alimony-getting rid of unwanted ex-spouses the painless, cost-free "PT": way. In other words, I was picking up your chips, leaving the jurisdiction, and disappearing.

A later report was about getting citizenship; Getting a new name and passport in Portugal. That too was very easy to do in those days. Unfortunately, it's no longer "instant" nor easy anymore. But it still can be done.

Then came my excellent little special report on how to make money by buying and fixing up the run-down property. That "portable trade" still works almost anywhere. Still, another book was "Sex Havens," all about "Instantly Finding the Illusion of Love in Thailand."

Even if you were seventy, in 3rd World Bangkok or Manila, it was (and still is) easy to get a gorgeous girlfriend or wife – if that is your thing.

Like all my "literary" works, these were self-published under different pen names. The books recounted the things I did. I told ordinary people how they could do the same. I always changed names to protect my anonymity. And my books and reports always brought in a few consulting clients who needed adult supervision.

MY BRIEF CAREER AS A DON JUAN AND HOW IT ENDED

Somewhere along the way, I decided to be a consultant to men attracting beautiful women from developing countries. To jump-start my new chosen profession, I contacted the then master of helping people find a third world girlfriend or wife:

The late Paradise Shelton had developed a way to profit and have a good life himself by helping lonely guys latch on to better women than they could ever hope to snag in their home countries. He simply chartered a yacht to visit the Pacific Islands- mostly the Philippines. His boats were usually filled with plumbers and tradespeople types. These were often guys without too much charm.

Shelton visited Islands and Atolls, where most local men had gone off to sea as sailors. There were ten or more hot, often gorgeous young unmarried women for every man. A garbage collector from Berlin or Chicago was considered a good catch for these girls. The lonely women tried very hard to please their visiting future husbands-to-be.

Ahhh, the years spent recruiting those nubile, young, and tan, barefoot beauties were a high point in my life. I will always remember the fringe benefits on those trips to Southeast Asia. Today such consulting still can be, and is, done on the Internet.

Eventually, I got snagged myself- by one of the best prospective 3rd World Brides I'd encountered. But settling in with a little brown girl in a little grass shack (for a while) is not the worst thing that could happen. I never regretted it. Twenty years later, I am with the same woman! Moving on in our story.

WHAT ABOUT THE SIX FLAGS?

Residence,
Citizenship,
Playgrounds,
Offshore Asset Placement,
Physical business Locations
An Internet Consulting Business.

For a complete summary of the six flags, go to FreedomPrivacyWealth.com

I had already realized that anyone could use the six flags. But at the time, I didn't think anyone could make a living by being a PT consultant.

Was I wrong! A gentleman named Harry Schultz made it very big. Schultz was listed for 30 years in the Guinness Book of World Records as the highest-paid consultant in the World!

PT consulting eventually became a massive industry with many topical books and newsletters. There are currently around 35,000 PT related adverts and products listed on the Net. Unfortunately, just like authors of the "Get Rich Quick" books, most of those advertisers know little or nothing about actually living the PT life. They are "All Hat & No Cattle," as the old boys in Texas used to say.

Unfortunately, most "How To" books are written by "know-nothings" and/or plagiarized from others.

However, once you know what you are doing and have done it yourself, selling the PT Philosophy still is an excellent way to make money, enjoy forbidden pleasures, cheap booze, fantastic, uninhibited, unlimited love and sex, pay less taxes, and be paid to travel to fascinating places. As a PT, consultant, or otherwise, you'll have a much better life than ordinary mortals.

Most people are struggling along in an unpleasant, stressful rat race. It usually takes a crisis like a divorce, lawsuit, or wrongful criminal indictment for them even to consider the delightful alternatives of the six flags. There's a banquet going on, and they don't even know where the table is.

There are several excellent consultants around these days, and enough biz to keep us very busy. Other good consultants do the same thing in their respective fields as I did for the PT world. They have specialties like Offshore Investing, Getting Foreign Residences, 2nd Passports, and Noble Titles. Another big niche is Arranging For 3rd World Marriages, etc.

HIGH PROFILE - TO BE AVOIDED

Especially where several countries are or can be involved in a business, there are legal opportunities for generating paper losses in nations where taxes are high. One rings the cash register to show profits only where taxes are low or non-existent. Nevertheless, to avoid being targeted, tax avoidance activities should be kept a low profile.

If you are a consultant tax planner, to the extent your own ego allows, it is better to keep your own name and photo out of the public media. However, being a low profile professional consultant who arranges these things can be immensely profitable. We have found that publicized success leads to investigative reporters, tax collectors, and assorted con men swarming around you like sharks are drawn to blood. However, all the large corporations like Facebook, Google, Microsoft are the same in this regard. International Tax Consultants arrange their affairs so that they pay a tax of close to zero on huge revenues. Many years ago, I was a member of the International Association of Tax Planners for a while. I only quit being a consultant in this field because forming corporations, setting up bank accounts, and pushing paper profits and losses around was not my idea of a good time. If you want to learn this profitable business, ask us at (FreedomPrivacyWealth.com) to refer to an expert we know.

CAN YOU BREAKAWAY, BECOME A PT, AND MAKE A LOT OF MONEY?

Of course, you can. If the dumb guys I know can become multi-millionaires, anyone reading this can make it too. Why? Because to get this far (in reading my little report) , you've already shown more intelligence than the average millionaire. Intelligence is an advantage. Goals, information, knowledge, and judgment are the imperatives.

GETTING BACK TO THE SPECIFICS OF WRITING AN INFORMATIVE BOOK:

Write from experience, not ignorance.

Be completely honest with your readers and clients.

Never encourage any criminal or fraudulent actions. That can get you into serious hot water. Readers or clients will finger you as their "criminal mastermind."

When you write, I suggest you never hold back any useful information. At the same time, be careful about sharing anything info the reader might get himself into trouble with. A little knowledge can be a dangerous thing.

Show the reader how much you know and how sincere and honest you are.

No matter how much you tell them, some readers (if you invite further inquiries) will want you personally to apply your expertise to their personal situations. About 3-5% of book buyers will probably become consulting customers.

When you start out, of course, you might consider a more competitive rate. Higher fees come only with experience and reputation.

When I like a new client, personal meetings are included at no extra charge aside from travel costs. Typically, we become social friends.

WHAT TO CHARGE FOR YOUR BOOKS OR CONSULTATIONS?

Experiment! Negotiate! Be flexible at first. Always offer an unconditional money back guaranty. This will overcome predictable resistance to relatively high prices.

Nobody ever asked me for a refund. Why?
Simply because I always did a good job of addressing their needs.

WHAT ELSE DOES A CONSULTANT DO?

I give hope and confidence. I keep or get clients out of trouble. I help clients achieve their goals and generally keep them happy. We often discover and explore options the client never knew existed-- or was too scared to try.

A CURE FOR STUPIDITY?

John Wayne said,
"Life is tough, but it's even tougher if you're stupid."

I often have to insist loudly that my clients avoid foolish actions. One American client "secretly" moved from New York to Hawaii. It's always a mistake to hide in the same country where the enemy is after you! From Hawaii, he regularly taunted his alimony drone ex-wife in New York on the telephone. He called her from his own home (an even bigger mistake). Of course, her hired investigator was able to trace him. Her lawyers attached his Hawaii property. His goose was cooked.

Another chap who was settled in England bragged to his ex that he had an account in Liechtenstein, and she couldn't touch it. Wrong! Once she knew where her husband's money was on deposit, she was able to seize it with the help of the Liechtenstein courts. Bank secrecy only protects those who can keep a secret.

Many clients lack common sense. Some won't take your good advice. But you must try your best to put them on the right path firmly yet diplomatically. Never get angry at them. (Yes, I do get annoyed and even angry when clients won't take advice and do silly things that can get them into trouble. But I try to keep cool.) After all, life is a do it yourself project, and if they insist on doing things the wrong way, well, I did my best, and they need to suffer the consequences.

HOW MUCH TO CHARGE

I charge €15,000 for two years of unlimited but reasonable consulting. This seems high for some clients a bargain to others. But as a consultant, you need to charge more than nickels and dimes because one on one consulting is labor-intensive. It is very time-consuming to provide personal services. My fees are probably under 10% of what any hotshot lawyer would charge. I was a lawyer before I decided I didn't like lawyers or being what they all are: "Officers of the Courts and Representatives of their particular Big Brother Government." They seldom put the client's needs first. My clients wouldn't get nearly as good results (and as many options) from a lawyer. Further, a domestic lawyer works for the Government first, and the client secondly.

Experiment with fees and maybe even do some "pro bono" work to gain experience.

DANGER!

These days, reporting requirements make local lawyers, bankers, and accountants into government informants. They can't give the best advice without risking an indictment for "conspiracy." They may have to return "Tainted Money" fees they accepted in good faith.

There is also a significant risk that your first consulting client may get himself into trouble (or even be a criminal!). If you are not careful, your client, when caught, will then try to extricate himself by wrongly fingering/blaming you as the mastermind behind his blunders. There are ways to protect against this, but I will save that info for paying clients. Hint: Being in a different jurisdiction from your client helps . . .

CONSULTING FOR THE MASS MARKET
To attract a less affluent, much broader client base, I suggest this:

Put your ideas in print, on video DVD or audio disk. It only costs $2-$5 for a plastic DVD and an attractive cover. Then you can profit as Microsoft does. Your advice on plastic or in print can be sold for $100, $250, or whatever the traffic will bear. Yet the cost of replication is nominal. Instead of spending many hours with a client, you pay a shipper (like Mail Boxes, Etc.) a small handling charge to receive and fill orders. A profitable niche is to sell $200 home study refresher courses to people who are legally required to take them (i.e., most professions and trades), and you will make serious money – hand over fist.

Experiment and advertise. In the unlikely event that you sell too much too fast, your prices are probably too low. They should be raised. If you sell anything, your price is too high. Or maybe you are not promoting correctly. Perhaps you just don't have a product or service that people want. Create a niche to differentiate yourself from the competition. Target a market (i.e., people!) needing your products or services that are not currently being served.

TO AVOID DISAPPOINTED CUSTOMERS, ALWAYS OFFER AN UNCONDITIONAL REFUND. ASK ANY CUSTOMER [who makes unhappy noises] HOW YOU CAN put a smile on their face...

DO WHATEVER IT TAKES TO SERVICE ANY UNHAPPY CUSTOMER. GIVE THEM WHAT THEY WANT OR NEED. Satisfied customers are your best source of referral to new business.

If you get more than 5% refund requests, find out why. Then go back to the drawing boards. You are doing something wrong.

To learn about marketing from a master, look on the web for "Jay Abraham." He has lots of free material. Jay may even partner with you to promote your products or services. There are many outfits telling you how to market things. Unfortunately, most of them only sell lousy advice and don't know what they are talking about. On Google Internet search, look up "The Rich Jerk." He's another successful marketer.

REPLICATION of your knowledge in print, video, audio, etc. is one of the best ways to sell a tangible course or product. It will lead qualified customers to your personal consulting services –or other related products or services. In our field, this is called "The Back End." You provide one product or service and then offer related stuff.

DON'T SERVICE ALL POTENTIAL CLIENTS!

One of the more admirable consulting features is you can always reject contact with potential clients you don't like – for instance, crooks- who might bring unwanted heat. If anyone causes you discomfort or trouble, just make a full refund and fire them. You are not dependent upon one "Boss." Clients should be more like students. You are a respected professor.

YOU CAN DO IT FROM ANYWHERE!

Another plus is that consulting is a portable trade....

Using the Net or Skype free phones, you can be on a beach in a tax-free Shangri La- on the other side of the World from your clients. You can get plenty of books and info by Googling "How to Become a Consultant" and similar phrases.

Many free online catalogs and a lot of inexpensive info are written by people who sell consulting services as a back end product to readers. Many people will buy your books if they are in such a catalog.

You might do a new revised version of an existing "how-to" book that is long out of copyright and sells it to others. In that way, you can become a consultant. I do emphasize you should know your stuff! Clients who discover you are incompetent or know less than they do will not be happy.

Please don't follow my exact modus operandi. Develop your own variant if you want to be successful. I describe the techniques here because they work for me. You will make it as a Consultant with your own niche products and your own original marketing variations.

CONSULTING IS GENERALLY UNREGULATED!

Anyone can be a consultant in almost any field without any permits or licenses.

It can be done on the net or from any location.

If you really know your stuff, you can be a consultant like me.

I hope this little push helps you achieve your goals.

HOW TO LIVE TAX-FREE (AND STRESS-FREE) FOR THE REST OF YOUR LIFE

Once you are Independently Wealthy with at least £175,00 or $250,000 in assets ...)

The following material you might consider a commercial for my other books, but the plain fact is that once I solved the problem of poverty, new dangers and needs arose. How I coped, survived, and came out sane, and the solvent was the subject of several other books that could help you. I regard PT as the best book because it is the keystone that ties the whole puzzle of life together. Think Like a Tycoon and Insider Secrets is about how to make money. The other PT books will show you how to enjoy it and keep it from the many predators and villains who want to steal it from you.

Do you want to escape the control over your life and property now held by the current Big Brother government? THE "PT" concept could have been called Individual Sovereignty because PTs look after themselves. We don't want or need authorities dominating every aspect of our existence from the cradle to the grave. The PT concept is one way to break free.

In a nutshell, a PT merely arranges his or her "paperwork" in such a way that all governments consider him a tourist - a person who is just "Passing Through" The advantage is that by being thought of by government officials as a person who is merely "Parked Temporarily," a PT is not subjected to taxes, military service, lawsuits, or persecution for partaking in innocent but forbidden pursuits or pleasures. Unlike most citizens or subjects, the PT will not be persecuted for his beliefs or lack of them. PT stands for many things: a PT can be a "Prior Taxpayer," "Perpetual Tourist," or "Permanent Traveler" if he or she wants to be. The individual who is a PT can stay in one place most of the time. Or all of the time! PT is a concept, a way of life, a way of perceiving the universe and your place in it. One can be a full-time, dedicated PT or a part-time PT. Some budding Tycoons may not want to break out at once or become a PT at all. They just want to be aware of the possibilities and be prepared to cash in their chips and modify their lifestyle in the event of a crisis. Knowledge will make you sort of a PT - a "Possibility Thinker" who is "Prepared Thoroughly" for the future.

The PT concept is elegant, simple, and requires no accountants, attorneys, offshore corporations, or other complex arrangements. Since the income of most PTs is immediately doubled, and most frustrations of life with Big Brother is instantly eliminated; the logical question is only:

Can you afford not to become a PT?

Unlimited, untaxed wealth, and the power to dispose of it as you please is one of the significant benefits of becoming a PT. PTs can work and be paid in full (without withholding tax or deductions) and then spend our earnings on what gives us pleasure. Until you become a PT, the range of opportunities denied you is inconceivable. We don't miss the things we are unaware of. PT, the book, will raise your consciousness of the nature of freedom and the ways to rid yourself of all limitations. Most nations' constitutions give lip-service to the absolute freedom to travel, but in practice, every Government severely limits travel with a passport, visa, and other requirements.

By imposing restrictions on foreigners, most nations invite tit-for-tat reciprocal measures. Personal finances, currency controls, domestic situations, and job requirements make the freedom to go anywhere at any time, just a dream for most people. Once properly equipped, the PT operates above and outside of normal constraints, gaining mobility and a full slate of human rights. The value of these rights cannot even be perceived by people who have never experienced them.

You don't need to found a new country or displace someone to make yourself a sovereign. The PT need not dominate other people. He or she must only be willing to break out of a parochial way of thinking: the PT must be superior only in that small area located between the ears. We speak of the potential PT now in terms of wealth, talent, intelligence, and creativity. Who is this PT in the upper minuscule of the population? It might well be you . . .

INFORMATIONAL AND INSPIRATIONAL BOOKS

By Dr. W.G. HILL

For Seekers of Freedom, Privacy, and Wealth
By THE SOVEREIGN LIFE REPORT
THE FIVE GREATEST BOOKS OF ALL TIME

PT: THE PERPETUAL TRAVELLER - by W. G. Hill.
Go to W. G. Hills Official website to read the full article.

The Historical Works of W. G. Hill
The original cost of these PT books was over $1,000.

The famous out of print collector's 1985 Classic Edition of the original

PT "Perpetual Traveler" by W.G. Hill and Harry Schultz.

The ultimate way to avoid government control of your life and your property is to become invisible. Ideally, you should never "belong" to anyone's government. Big Brother should never know; who you are, where you live, how you make your money, where you keep your assets, and perhaps most important, where you like to "play."

PT a Coherent for a Stress-free Healthy and Prosperous Life Without Government Interference, Taxes, or Coercion.

The philosophy behind these ideals is to become a "PT," a Perpetual Tourist, Parked Temporarily, a Prior Taxpayer who is now a Possibility Thinker, and Prepared Thoroughly for the future.

Insider Secrets - Become A Successful Entrepreneur

This Unconventional Guide is for seasoned entrepreneurs as well as beginners in the biz. Insider Secrets will show you how To Become Successful Anywhere In The World. The Insider Secrets is the Only

Resources You Will Ever Need that will show you how to use your overlooked skills and how you can get into the mindset of highly successful business people. Do you want to learn the secrets that made many smart thinking entrepreneurs become wealthy tycoons? No college degrees or licenses are required to build your Empire. Start today!

No Worries About Permits, Licenses, or Regulations!

The Monaco Report

How To Become a Legal Resident of Tax-Free Monte Carlo, Monaco
There are a few problems in paradise, one of them being the French Government. But for those who read this Special Report, the effect of French fiscal measures can be entirely and legally avoided.

The report also goes into how to earn a living, manage a business, handle investments, form corporations or trusts, etc.

Campione Confidential

How to Get Legal Residence in the Tax Haven of Campione For the cost of renting an apartment, you can get an ID card and lifetime Swiss driving license. This allows you to travel anywhere in Europe as the equivalent of a dual citizen of Italy and Switzerland. Visas to anywhere are easy to get for Campione residents.

Le Livre Du Corps Diplomatique -
"How To Become an Honorary Consul General"

An honorary diplomat is generally appointed by countries that cannot afford or do not wish to spend the substantial amounts required to set up an office. Appointing an honorary consul saves them the cost of supporting staff and sending out their citizens as full-time diplomatic representatives abroad.

This Honorary Consul Report, written by W.G. Hill, the number one

PT, was initially sold for the US $10.000 per copy to a very selective small number of clients, all of whom were successfully appointed as honorary diplomats.

Think Like a Tycoon

> How To Make A Million In Three Years Or Less
> Profit From Selling Distressed Properties

This is not a get-rich-quick book with "magic" formulas and "secret" potions that will make you a millionaire overnight. If you are looking for a real-world financial guide that will allow you to:

> √ Build Your Fortune Step-By-Step
> √ Learn How To Profit From Inflation
> √ Change Your Mindset and Become A Tycoon

This report is designed to give the reader the practical knowledge and essential skills needed to make money and obtain credit through the property. It will show you that buying and selling property is the easiest and quickest way to make a fortune. 'Think Like a Tycoon' sets out a two to three-year plan to financial independence. Follow the guidelines in the report, and you could be a millionaire in two years.

INTRODUCTION

"Grandpa," the former editor at both Global Publishing & Scope Books Investor, entrepreneur, ex-lawyer, published author, live in Monaco. "Grandpa" is the author of Bye Bye Big Brother and dozens of other PT books.

He is a very experienced Octogenarian, successful stock market, and real estate investor. A retired lawyer is now living as a PT with "flags" in Monaco, Switzerland, Argentina, and the Philippines. He has helped people get amicable divorces, a residence, and citizenship in several Central American and European countries.

Instant Legal Residence Abroad

What's the truth? That spending serious money is not necessary!

In places like Latvia, you can get instant EU residence for a small €75,000 investment in five €15,000 apartments that will bring you up to a 100% annual return on your money. All explained in this exciting new "Grandpa" report. In places like Campione, you can get residence and the equivalent of both a Swiss and an Italian passport, plus free or cheap medical insurance, for the price of renting a cheap studio apartment.

ESCAPE!

ESCAPE! is a report for EVERYONE who wants to be free, or just to stay out of trouble. The current world system intends to leave no human beings outside of the "collective." Big Brother wants you to have no way to checkout; no way out of their game! Once you are registered as "belonging" to one State, that State retains a controlling interest in you for the rest of your life — cradle to grave.

> IN THIS SPECIAL REPORT, WE WILL SHOW YOU
> HOW TO FLY UNDER THE RADAR FOREVER!

Bye Bye Big Brother

The Bye Bye Big Brother and the earlier PT books" are about leaving one's mother country for more happy-making, desirable places. They cover how to make a good living in your new home -- abroad. If you want to make successful choices that you will be happy with, I suggest you purchase and read those books (at least Bye Bye Big Brother) first.

We regard these as another source of inspiration for PTs and recommend them most highly! Bridge Across Forever and Jonathan Livingston Seagull, by Richard Bach, published by William Morrow, New York. The international best-seller is available in most bookstores.

How I Found Freedom in an Unfree World, Harry Brown, published by Avon Books, 959 Eighth Avenue, NYC, USA. How to Retire at Age 35 by Roger Terhorst, Bantam Books Paperbacks available in bookstores. Free to Choose, Milton Freidman, also published by Avon Books.

Years ago, we got these questions from new PT readers.

"There are many PT books and reports around, are there any chronology suggestions that would make becoming a PT and navigation slightly more coherent for me?"

"I read many books on similar topics, but the whole PT idea is still new to me. Should I start by reading the original "historical books" in Hill collection? ****YES!****, or should I jump right to Bye Bye Big Brother (I.E., does BBBB make the Hill set redundant or outdated)?"

If you are short on time, read Bye Bye Big Brother first. Otherwise, bone up in chronological; order with the "Historic Hill Collection" first

In the PT world, info can be outdated by new laws the day it comes out. If you want to understand how and why things are, and where the future will take you, it is a very good idea to understand the way things were in the past.

Older PT books are not meant to be up to date regarding all specific new laws and details. It is all "historic & timeless classic. However, a few of the books have got a facelift or new material added to reflect changes.

For instance, The Passport Report pre-dates 9-11. After 9-11, Big Brother used "terrorism" as an excuse to shut down almost all reasonably priced foreign 2nd Passport Programs.

That is why we still sell the "Historic PT Collection" by W.G. Hill.
These books & reports started the PT movement in the '80s.
Later, Grandpa books and reports have updated this.
But the old (or updated) PT books might be just what you need?

Hopefully, you have enjoyed this book and will drop us a note letting us know how you felt about it. Please leave your comment on the Amazon book page or other book sites such as GoodRead.com and our own book page on my Official Site: PTsecrets WEB. We look forward to reading your review. How can we improve on later versions? In any event, I hope this book will help you get where you want to be!

Sincerely yours,
Dr. WG HILL

Questions, comments, corrections?
Contact the publisher:
support@FreedomPrivacyWealth.com

Join our discussion forums for PTs
- the PT Club and the PT Refuge -
You will find more details on the six flags,
the PT philosophy, and the PT books,
and plenty of free reading material at
W.G. Hill's Official Site, PTsecrets WEB
< www.FreedomPrivacyWealth.com >

www.ingramcontent.com/pod-product-compliance
Lightning Source LLC
Chambersburg PA
CBHW072236230526
45466CB00024B/2070